Fifth Grade Writing Prompts for Seasons:
A Creative Writing Workbook

Bryan Cohen

Edited by Ashley Daoust.

DEDICATION

I dedicate this book to spring, summer, fall and winter vacation and the countdown that goes along with each for both adults and children.

CONTENTS

INTRODUCTION

Welcome to the *Writing Prompts for Seasons* workbook series! Within these pages you'll find 200 writing prompts, two on each page, that will stimulate the imagination of your students or children. I've found that the key to allowing students to fully latch onto an idea is to give them a scenario followed by a question. In answering the question, young writers can take the same prompt a million different directions. You may even want to try photocopying a page and have your writers take on the same prompt at the beginning and the end of a school year, just to see how different their storytelling has become.

The *Writing Prompts for Seasons* series is a collection of books I've created after seeing how many parents and teachers have visited my website, Build Creative Writing Ideas (located at http://www.build-creative-writing-ideas.com). The most popular pages on my site coincide with prompts about the four seasons of spring, summer, fall and winter. I imagine this means two things: teachers and parents are searching for seasonal writing activities, and children enjoy writing about the changing weather and the upcoming holidays. I hope that this series will meet both of those needs while inspiring creativity in the minds of our youth. The five books in the series are available for grades 1, 2, 3, 4 and 5. The prompts become more complex with each volume, but continue to remain imaginative and creative throughout.

I love hearing about the progress of students on my site and I'm always interested in hearing new ideas for delivering creative writing prompts to writers from the ages of 5 to 105. Feel free to contact me on my website with any questions and comments you can think of. I hope you and your future best-selling authors thoroughly enjoy this and other books in the series. Happy writing!

Sincerely,
Bryan Cohen
Author of *Writing Prompts for Seasons*

PS: While there is space below each prompt for your budding writers to write, there is a good chance they may have more to say than they can fit on the page. There is an extra page in the back if you'd like to photocopy it, but I strongly suggest that you also get a notebook and some extra pencils just in case. A dictionary for challenging words may also be helpful.

Name _____ Date _____

1. The poet William Carlos Williams once wrote, "In summer, the song sings itself." If summer were a song, what kind of song would it be and why? Do you think summer is more musical than other seasons? Why or why not?

_____

_____

_____

_____

_____

2. According to playwright Anton Chekhov, "people don't notice whether it's winter or summer when they're happy." Do you agree with him? Why or why not? Would you say that you're happier during summer than other seasons? Why or why not?

_____

_____

_____

_____

Name _____ Date _____

3. A character in Lisa Schroder's book *I Heart You, You Haunt Me* says that "books and summertime go together." Do you enjoy it when books are a part of your summer? Why or why not? If you had to choose one book to read during the warmest months, what would it be and why?

_____

_____

_____

_____

_____

4. Author George R.R. Martin said that summer friends melt away while winter friends are the ones that last. Imagine what it would be like if your summer friends met with your winter friends during a party. Would you spend more time with one group over the other? Why or why not?

_____

_____

_____

_____

Name _____ Date _____

5. Poet Raymond Duncan said, "A lot of parents pack up their troubles and send them off to summer camp." If you were a parent, do you think you'd enjoy sending your kids to camp for a month or two? Why or why not? What would you do with your spare time?

_____

_____

_____

_____

6. Lucy Maud Montgomery's well-known character Anne once wondered allowed what it would be like to live in a world in which it was always June. How would your life change if it was always June? What sorts of things would you miss out on? What would the benefits be?

_____

_____

_____

_____

Name _____ Date _____

7. Summer is often connected with youth in poetry and literature. Why do you think this is? How would summer be different for a younger person and an older person and why?

_____

_____

_____

_____

_____

8. Ralph Waldo Emerson said that "summer will have its flies." What would you say are some of the "flies" of summer, other than actual flies? Do you think the positive aspects of summer outweigh the negative aspects and why?

_____

_____

_____

_____

_____

Name _____ Date _____

9. Author and journalist Hal Borland referred to summer as a loan that
needs to be repaid in January. Imagine that you could actually borrow extra days of summer now
but that it would require you deal with extra days of winter. Would the trade-off be worth it? Why
or why not?

_____

_____

_____

_____

_____

10. Poet James Russell Lowell refers to summer as a luxury that everyone can afford. What are
some ways in which summer is like a free vacation? Do you think the season is wonderful enough
on its own that no additional trips or expenditures are needed? Why or why not?

_____

_____

_____

_____

Name _____ Date _____

11. In Bob Marley's song Sun is Shining, he says that summer makes you want to dance. Has summer ever made you want to move your feet? Why or why not? What kind of dance might summer inspire you to do and why?

_____

_____

_____

_____

12. The video game *Animal Crossing: Wild World* says that "we can't let the sun outshine us! We have to beam, too!" What do you think it means to beam like the sun? Who is someone you know who shines like the sun and why?

_____

_____

_____

_____

Name _____ Date _____

13. George Gershwin's song Summertime says, "Summertime, and the
living is easy." What are some of the easiest parts of summer living? What are the hardest parts?
Would you say that summer living is easier than living in other seasons? Why or why not?

_____

_____

_____

_____

14. Nat King Cole referred to summer as lazy, hazy, and crazy. What are some of summer's best
examples of laziness, haziness, and craziness? What are some of the adjectives you'd use to
describe the warm season and why?

_____

_____

_____

_____

Name _____ Date _____

15. The song Summer Nights from *Grease* recounts the summer
relationship of the two main characters with all their friends clamoring to tell them more. Imagine
that you had a crazy summer tale to tell. Which of your friends would want to hear as much about
it as possible and why? Would you spill the beans? Why or why not?

_____

_____

_____

_____

_____

16. In the movie *Happy Campers*, the character Wichita says that people don't change at summer
camp, they simply find out who they are and start to become that person. Would you agree that
the summer gives you a chance to figure out who you are? Why or why not? What have you
found out so far?

_____

_____

_____

_____

_____

8

Name _____ Date _____

17. The Beach Boys' song *Kokomo* refers to a tropical vacation through
the islands of Jamaica, Aruba, Bermuda, and, of course, Kokomo Island. Imagine that you could
be on the beach all summer long. What would you do all day long? Would you ever get sick of it?
Why or why not?

_____

_____

_____

_____

18. In the movie *Jaws*, the summer vacation on Amity Island is disrupted by the presence of a
great white shark. The movie was a major hit. Why do you think a concept that was so scary
ended up being so popular? What other scary summer situations do you think could make good
movies?

_____

_____

_____

_____

Name _____ Date _____

19. Surfing is a popular subject of many summer songs, even inspiring a
subculture of surf music such as the song *Wipeout*. Why do you think surfing and music go
together? What kind of music would you want playing when you went surfing and why?

_____

_____

_____

_____

20. What is your favorite summer movie or television show and why? What kind of character
would you be if you could play a part in that movie or show? Would you enjoy it? Why or why
not?

_____

_____

_____

_____

Name _____ Date _____

21. Iced tea was invented by Richard Blechynden, a tea plantation owner
who realized his tea was too hot during the 1904 World's Fair in St. Louis. He added ice and the
rest was history. What is your favorite summer beverage and why? If you could invent your own
summer drink, what would it be?

_____

_____

_____

_____

22. At the very same World's Fair, the ice cream cone became popular when a stand selling the
dessert ran out of dishes and took thin waffle wafers from a nearby Persian food stand. Do you
think it's important for different cultures and ideas to come together? Why or why not? What are
some things other than ice cream cones that could result from collaboration?

_____

_____

_____

_____

Name _____ Date _____

23. Dr. Willis H. Carrier developed the first modern air conditioner in 1902, which was originally meant to keep the paper from drying out at a printing press. Why do you think Carrier first thought of cooling paper before he thought of cooling humans? How do you think people coped with heat prior to air conditioning?

_____

_____

_____

_____

_____

24. In the summer of 2008, Michael Phelps became the first Olympian to win eight gold medals in one Olympic Games. What would it be like to be the best in the world at something? What would be the pros and what would be the cons? If you could pick one thing to be the best at, what would it be and why?

_____

_____

_____

_____

_____

Name _____ Date _____

25. At the age of 11, Frank Epperson invented the popsicle in 1905 when he accidentally left some soda and a stirring stick outside overnight. It froze, and over 100 years later, we're still thanking him for the treat. Do you think you could be an inventor? Why or why not? What kind of product would you create and why?

_____

_____

_____

_____

26. In the summer of 1853, head chef George Crum invented the potato chip completely by accident when trying to get back at a guest who kept sending his friend potatoes back to the kitchen. Why do you think accidents and other unintentional actions often create inventions? What is your favorite summer snack food and why?

_____

_____

_____

_____

Name _____ Date _____

27. Mary Wollstonecraft Shelley had a dream in the summer of 1816 that later became the story for *Frankenstein*. Have you ever said, done, or written something that you saw in a dream? If so, what was it and how did you use it? If not, what kind of creation do you think you could come up with in a dream and why?

_____

_____

_____

_____

_____

28. Benjamin Franklin conducted many of his experiments with lightning and electricity during the summers between 1747 and 1752, including the famous kite experiment. If you could come up with an experiment to try during the summer, what would it be and why? Would your experiment be as dangerous as Franklin's? Why or why not?

_____

_____

_____

_____

Name _____ Date _____

29. July is the top month for ice cream sales and was made into National Ice Cream Month in the 1980s by President Ronald Reagan. Imagine that you have been asked to hold a giant ice cream festival in your town to celebrate the month. What activities would you have available, what kinds of ice cream would you use and would people enjoy the celebration?

_____

_____

_____

_____

_____

30. Before the 1840s, there was no such thing as summer vacation for schools. Do you think that summer vacation is a positive thing? Why or why not? How would your life be different if you had school all year long and why?

_____

_____

_____

_____

_____

Name _____ Date _____

31. Woofstock, one of the largest outdoor festivals for dog lovers, takes place every summer in Toronto, Canada. Would you ever take a trip just so your dog could have a good time? Why or why not? What do you think a dog's favorite activity would be during the summer and why?

_____

_____

_____

_____

32. Madrid, Spain plays host to a huge water fight involving over 5,000 people carrying hoses and buckets every year. Describe what it would be like to be a part of such a huge and drenching event. How would you feel and why? Who would you take with you to the event?

_____

_____

_____

_____

Name _____ Date _____

33. There are many races held throughout the world during the summer,
but none quite like one found in Wales during August. Participants scuba dive while riding a bike
through a six-foot deep muddy bog. What strange extreme sport could you create in your own
town? Who do you think would win and why?

_____

_____

_____

_____

34. The Chap Olympiad takes place every summer in London and includes events such as
moustache wrestling, cucumber sandwich discus and umbrella jousting. What other strange events
might you create for such a competition? Would you have fun watching the competition? Why or
why not?

_____

_____

_____

_____

Name _____ Date _____

35. The tiny town of Buñol, Spain is the site of La Tomatina, a massive tomato-throwing fight on the last Wednesday of August every year. Would your parents enjoy being part of such an event? Why or why not? How well do you think they'd do if they were dropped into the middle of the wet and wild event and why?

_____

_____

_____

_____

36. Each July, South Korea holds the Boryeong Mud Festival replete with mud pools, mud slides and mud skiing. What would your family do if you came up to the front door covered in mud? Would you get in trouble? Why or why not?

_____

_____

_____

_____

Name _____ Date _____

37. The World Toe Wrestling Championships are held in Ashbourne, England every June. How do you think you'd train for a toe wrestling contest? Which athlete do you think would have the best shot of winning the competition and why?

_____

_____

_____

_____

38. Multiple cultures celebrate the Summer Solstice by jumping over a small fire for good luck. Why do you think this might not be such a good idea? What might you want to jump over instead and why?

_____

_____

_____

_____

Name _____ Date _____

39. The Edinburgh Fringe Festival, the largest arts festival in the world, includes comedy, dance, theatre, and music performed by people from all around the world. What artistic show would you create and bring to the festival if you could? What would people think of it and why?

_____

_____

_____

_____

40. The Running of the Bulls, held annually in Pamplona, Spain, is one of the most dangerous events in the world. Participants literally run away from six bulls that are released to charge through the streets. Why do you think people would want to be included in this event? Do you know anyone who would do it? Why would they get involved?

_____

_____

_____

_____

Name _____ Date _____

41. Describe the hottest you've ever been during the summertime. Where
were you, what were you doing, and who were you with? How did you beat the heat? How did it
feel to be that hot and why?

_____

_____

_____

_____

42. What do you think is the hottest place in the entire world? What precautions might you have
to take to keep yourself safe? How and why do you think people choose to live in a place like
that?

_____

_____

_____

_____

Name _____ Date _____

43. You and your family have discovered a treasure chest of gold on the beach using your trusty metal detector. What happens next? Do you get any special credit for it being your metal detector? Why or why not?

_____

_____

_____

_____

_____

44. Imagine that you've been stranded on a desert island during the hottest part of the year. What will you do to survive? Will you get rescued? Why or why not?

_____

_____

_____

_____

Name _____ Date _____

45. You have written and published a best-selling book called *The Secret to Summer*. What is it about? Why do people enjoy it so much? How does your life change after writing a best-seller?

_____

_____

_____

_____

46. If you could take a class to learn one skill during the summer, what would it be and why? How would you incorporate this new skill into your life? What would your friends think and why?

_____

_____

_____

_____

Name _____ Date _____

47. Your family has embarked on a 50-mile bike trip to explore everything your city has to offer. What places would you want to go to and why? Would the 50 miles be tough on you? Why or why not?

_____

_____

_____

_____

_____

48. You and some friends have purchased Around the World plane tickets for the summer, allowing you to visit multiple cities in every continent. What places would you most want to visit and why? What would you learn in getting to see so many different cultures and why?

_____

_____

_____

_____

Name _____ Date _____

49. Which of the following summer activities would you be most likely to do: relax by the poolside, go fishing, build a sand castle, run a lemonade stand, or read a book series? Why would you make that choice? How does that activity make you feel and why?

_____

_____

_____

_____

50. Create a made-up story using the following words: sandy, crabs, drenched, and mouthwatering.

_____

_____

_____

_____

Name _____ Date _____

51. William Cullen Bryant, a poet and journalist, said that autumn was "the year's last, loveliest smile." What does Bryant mean when he says it's the last smile of the year? Would you agree that it's the loveliest smile as well? Why or why not?

_____

_____

_____

_____

_____

52. Poet Percy Bysshe Shelley wrote about leaves falling from trees as if they were ghosts being driven away. How would the season be different if falling leaves actually were ghosts? How would raking be different? How would the ghostly leaves act and why?

_____

_____

_____

_____

_____

Name _____ Date _____

53. Fall is the "mellow time" according to Irish poet William Allingham.
Would you agree with him? What are some of the ways in which the fall is mellow for you? What are some ways in which it is the opposite? Which is the most mellow season for you and why?

_____

_____

_____

_____

_____

54. In George Cooper's poem "October's Party," the leaves, sunshine, weather, and wind all come to play in a giant celebration for the season. Imagine that all these things could walk and talk and dance. What would their fall party be like and why? How would it change if humans were invited and why?

_____

_____

_____

_____

Name _____ Date _____

55. The fall season may be cause for us to be sad and sympathetic for the trees that are losing all their leaves, according to poet Robert Browning. Create a conversation between a tree losing its leaves and yourself. Would the tree be sad? Why or why not? How would you describe the fall, winter, and spring to a tree that didn't understand?

_____

_____

_____

_____

_____

56. Sir Walter Scott, a Scottish poet, said that if a tree doesn't blossom in the spring, you certainly won't see fruit on it in the fall. Why do some people expect to get the "fruits" of success without putting in the necessary work first? What are some aspects of your life that require hard work first and why are they worth it?

_____

_____

_____

_____

Name _____ Date _____

57. There are people who would rather summer never end and transition into fall, according to author Hal Borland. These same people unsuccessfully hope the world will do exactly what they want. Why is it important to realize that some things are out of our control? How does it feel to accept that something is going to happen?

_____

_____

_____

_____

58. British humorist Thomas Hood said that many of the wonderful aspects of nature, including butterflies, fruits, flowers, and birds, were completely absent in November. Do you miss those aspects of nature as much as Hood? Why or why not? What are some of the more positive aspects of November?

_____

_____

_____

_____

Name _____ Date _____

59. Chuang Tzu, a 4th century Chinese philosopher, said that opinions are like autumn, gradually changing and passing away. How have your opinions changed in the last few years? How do you think they will change in the future? Do you think Chuang Tzu is right? Why or why not?

_____

_____

_____

_____

_____

60. According to Italian philosopher Umberto Eco, not only do opinions change, but the way we look changes like autumn as well. How do you think your looks will change as you get older? Which do you think is more important, what you have on the inside or what you have on the outside and why?

_____

_____

_____

_____

_____

Name _____ Date _____

61. Television producer and writer Mitchell Burgess said on the show
Northern Exposure that fall was a time for reflecting on the past. What are some of the ways that you look back at things that have happened in the past year? Do you think reflection is important? Why or why not?

_____

_____

_____

_____

62. The Kinks song Autumn Almanac lists all of the aspects of fall, from the colder weather to the musty yellow leaves, as things you have to deal with. If you made a list of everything that happened during the fall, how would it make you feel? Do the parts of the season you like make up for the parts you don't like? Why or why not?

_____

_____

_____

_____

Name _____ Date _____

63. In the movie *Planes, Trains, and Automobiles*, the main characters take any means necessary to get home for Thanksgiving. If you were stranded far away from home on turkey day, how would you try to get there? Would you take anyone with you for companionship? Why or why not?

_____

_____

_____

_____

_____

64. The narrator in the song Autumn by the Edgar Winter Group states that the birds don't have much to say in the fall because they know what's coming. How do you think birds and other animals feel about the post-summer season and why? Do they actually know what's coming? Why or why not?

_____

_____

_____

_____

Name _____ Date _____

65. The movie *October Sky* shows the character Homer Hickam become
inspired when he sees the first satellite launched into space during the fall. Have you ever seen
something in the sky that inspired you? If so, what was it and why did it make you feel that way?
If not, what would be something that you might see in the sky that could motivate you and why?

_____

_____

_____

_____

66. The song October by U2 states that even though Kingdoms rise and fall, October will continue
to go on. How do you think the world will change in the next few hundred years while October
stays the same? While it change for the better? Why or why not?

_____

_____

_____

_____

Name _____ Date _____

67. Many inspirational sports movies like *Remember the Titans, Hoosiers,*
and *Rudy* are set during the fall. If you could write your own touching fall sports tale, what sport
would it be about, what would happen to the main character and why would people enjoy it?

_____

_____

_____

_____

_____

68. The narrator in Justin Hayward's song Forever Autumn says that he wishes he could migrate
south with the birds after his love left him. What would the fall be like if you were able to fly
along with the birds and go south for the winter? How would living with the birds be different
than living at home and why?

_____

_____

_____

_____

Name _____ Date _____

69. In multiple films, poems, and songs, autumn is referred to as a time
when adults are getting older and winding down their lives. How do you think your parents will
spend their later years of retirement and why? How will you spend your retirement years and
why?

_____

_____

_____

_____

70. In Van Morrison's When the Leaves Come Falling Down, the narrator talks to a girl who
thinks about "the wisdom of the leaves and their grace." Would you consider leaves wise and full
of grace? Why or why not? How would you describe leaves and why?

_____

_____

_____

_____

Name _____ Date _____

71. Elias Howe obtained the first patent for a sewing machine in
September, 1846. How would the world be different if everybody still stitched clothing by hand?
What are some of the ways that sewing machines large and small are used today?

_____

_____

_____

_____

_____

72. In the fall of 1900, Orville and Wilbur Wright began experimenting with their first airplane in
the beach town of Kitty Hawk, North Carolina. Imagine that you were in the tiny gliding plane on
the first test drive. Would you be scared? Why or why not? What do you think people living in the
year 1900 might think of their invention and why?

_____

_____

_____

_____

Name _____ Date _____

73. Tools similar to the rake were used in China in 1100 B.C.E. to harvest hay and grain. What do you think it would have been like to deal with outdoor chores over 3,000 years ago? What would your excuses be to get out of the work and why?

_____

_____

_____

_____

74. In the early 1970s, the rake was replaced in some garages by the world's first power leaf blower. Consumers actually modified an insect spray device by removing the tank and the company began to realize they had leaf-blowing gold on their hands. What are some other tools that you think should be replaced by technology? What would the replacements do better and why?

_____

_____

_____

_____

Name _____ Date _____

75. Germany became the first country to use daylight savings time in 1916, allowing us to spring forward and fall back. What are some ways in which you could use the extra hour given to us during the fall other than sleeping? Why would this be a good use of your extra time?

_____

_____

_____

_____

_____

76. In the fall of 2008, a team of Oxford University scientists revived an old refrigerator design patented by Albert Einstein in November, 1930. Even though it was created more than 70 years earlier, the design was thought to be more environmentally friendly. What are some ideas from the past that you think could or should be brought back to the present and why?

_____

_____

_____

_____

_____

Name _____ Date _____

77. Sir Isaac Newton helped to develop the beginnings of modern mathematics in the fall of 1666 with what would later be called calculus. Why do you think creating an advanced system of math would be important? What are some things that might not have been invented if it wasn't for advanced calculus?

_____

_____

_____

_____

_____

78. The first jack-o'-lanterns could be found in Ireland but they were made of turnips, potatoes, and beets as opposed to pumpkins. What do you think would be the strangest fruit or vegetable to use for a jack-o'-lantern? What kind of face would you carve into it and why?

_____

_____

_____

_____

_____

Name _____ Date _____

79. It took over 200 years for Thanksgiving to become a national holiday, after Abraham Lincoln declared it officially in 1863. What other famous events from U.S. history should be made into national holidays? When would they be celebrated and what would some of the celebratory traditions be?

_____

_____

_____

_____

_____

80. The first official fall football game was played in 1869 between the College of New Jersey (now Princeton University) and the Rutgers University. How different do you think the game might have been from the sport we watch today? How might a star from today do if he or she played back in 1869 and why?

_____

_____

_____

_____

Name _____ Date _____

81. Munich, Germany is the host to one of the largest fall festivals in the world, Oktoberfest. Attendees drink from giant mugs or glass boots and eat delicious sausages. Imagine that you have created a festival for a different month (such as Septemberfest). What kind of event would it be, what activities would be available, and what types of food could you get there?

_____

_____

_____

_____

_____

82. November 5 is a public holiday in London to commemorate a failed attempt on the king's life by a man named Guy Fawkes. Guy Fawkes Night is filled with fireworks, costume parties, and burning effigies of Guy Fawkes. Have you ever been notorious for something? If so, what was it for and how did you try to clear your name? If not, what might it feel like for someone to think you were the bad guy or girl?

_____

_____

_____

_____

Name _____ Date _____

83. Mexico is known in the fall for its early November celebration of Day of the Dead. Families celebrate the lives of their deceased relatives with candies, parties and dancing. What would it be like if there was a similar holiday celebrated in the United States? Would it feel strange to dance and sing in a cemetery? Why or why not?

_____

_____

_____

_____

84. The White Night is a celebration in Paris, France on the night of October 1 in which all museums, monuments and tourist attractions stay open all night and are accompanied by bright lights and music. If you found yourself in France for the festival, how many different places would you try to see? Which might you enjoy the most and why?

_____

_____

_____

_____

Name _____ Date _____

85. Jodhpur, India hosts the Rajasthan International Folk Festival every October, bringing together more than 100 musicians from around the world. Do you think it's important to experience music from different cultures? Why or why not? What country's music would you want to see the most at a festival like RIFF and why?

_____

_____

_____

_____

86. Not all international events happen in a physical place. Filminute, an international one-minute film festival, happens online throughout the month of September. As technology continues to improve, do you think that more events will be held online? Why or why not? Would you rather go to an event in person or online and why?

_____

_____

_____

_____

Name _____ Date _____

87. The last Sunday of every November is the annual Monkey Buffet
Festival in Lopburi, Thailand. The festival is a literal feeding frenzy for the many monkeys who
live in the area. What kind of animal do you think your town would feed instead of monkeys
during an animal food festival and why? What would be the most difficult part about putting it
together and why?

_____

_____

_____

_____

_____

88. Approximately 300,000 people and 20,000 camels gather every November for the Pushkar
Camel Fair in Pushkar, India. Describe what it might look like to ride a camel through the festival.
Imagine how the fair would be decorated and write out the possible details.

_____

_____

_____

_____

_____

Name _____ Date _____

89. Sydney, Australia is the site for the Crave Sydney International Food Festival every October. Top international chefs and visitors come to the city to cook and taste the best of Australian cuisine. Imagine that you were hosting a party with a menu created by chefs from around the world. What different cultures would you and your friends feast on and why?

_____

_____

_____

_____

_____

90. In October, the city of Bacolod, Philippines hosts the Masskara Festival in which over 400,000 people wear brightly colored masks. Imagine that you could disguise yourself with a mask that made everybody think you were someone else. What person would you pretend to be and why? What would you do while everyone thought you weren't you? Why?

_____

_____

_____

_____

45

Name _____ Date _____

91. While picking apples, your family has decided to compete to see who
can get the most in an hour. How do you ensure that your basket is fullest by the end of the hour?
Who in your family do you think would win and why?

_____

_____

_____

_____

_____

92. What do you think is the secret ingredient to a perfect fall apple pie? If you successfully used
this ingredient, would you tell people the secret? Why or why not? What are some recipes you
know that use secret ingredients?

_____

_____

_____

_____

_____

Name _____ Date _____

93. In a major sight to see, all of the jack-o'-lanterns on your block have grown orange legs and started marching down the street. What happens next? Do you ever find a cause for this phenomenon? Why or why not?

_____

_____

_____

_____

94. Do you think you will enjoy pumpkins as much when you're an adult as you do now and why? How much do your parents like pumpkins and why?

_____

_____

_____

_____

Name _____ Date _____

95. You have been commissioned to create a fall festival for your school
or neighborhood. Who do you bring on to help you and why? What role does everybody play in
the planning process and why?

_____

_____

_____

_____

_____

96. What would be the most important aspects of this fall festival and why? What would be the
activities for the adults and what would the kids do for fun? What kinds of food would be there
and why?

_____

_____

_____

_____

Name _____ Date _____

97. Because of Halloween, fall is a time for extremely scary movies. Do you have a favorite kind of scary movie? Why or why not? Are there certain kinds of scary movies you won't watch? Why?

_____

_____

_____

_____

_____

98. Fall is also the time for starting a brand new year of school. What are some of the feelings you have at the start of a school year and why? Do you think other people feel those feelings too? Why or why not?

_____

_____

_____

_____

Name _____ Date _____

99. Create a made-up story using the following words: foliage, pumpkin patch, frightening, and backpack.

_____

_____

_____

_____

_____

100. If you were to carve a different jack-o'-lantern to represent different members of your family, what would they look like and why? Make sure to go into great detail for each one and to explain what each member would think of them.

_____

_____

_____

_____

_____

Name _____ Date _____

101. A proverbial saying related to winter states that a rich man gets his
ice in the summer and a poor man gets his in the winter. What do you think that means and why?
What other things might a poor person not be entitled to that a rich person could have all year
long?

_____

_____

_____

_____

102. In the 16th century, winter was used in literature as a symbol of old age. In what ways does
winter make you think about aging? If you were writing a poem about winter, would you use
winter to symbolize something different? Why or why not?

_____

_____

_____

_____

Name _____ Date _____

103. Shakespeare's play *A Winter's Tale* sets half of the play in the winter
during the reign of the cold-hearted King Leontes. Do you think that some people act differently
during the winter? Why or why not? Might these same people literally become warm emotionally
during the warmer months? Why or why not?

_____

_____

_____

_____

_____

104. The phrase lion in winter, used as the title of James Goldman's play *The Lion in Winter*,
refers to a strong and important person who has become old and less important because of age and
hardship. Do you think that you will get better with age? Why or why not? Why might it be tough
to be strong when you reach a certain age?

_____

_____

_____

_____

Name _____ Date _____

105. *Richard III*, another Shakespearian play, refers to a time of
unhappiness as "the winter of our discontent." Have you ever had a winter of discontent? If so,
what made your winter so unhappy and why? If not, imagine and write about what you would
have to do to get yourself out of a winter funk.

_____

_____

_____

_____

106. George Herbert, a poet famous for his pattern poems, once wrote that "every mile is two in
winter." What might he mean literally and figuratively by that? What are some of the aspects of
winter that seem long and why?

_____

_____

_____

_____

Name _____ Date _____

107. British poet Edith Sitwell wrote that winter is a time for home. Why do you think home is especially important during the winter? Imagine that you had to spend winter far away from home. How would it be different?

_____

_____

_____

_____

108. Anne Bradstreet, who wrote the first book by a woman that was published in the United States, wrote that "if we had no winter, the spring would not be so pleasant." Would you agree with that statement? Do we need to have the unhappy side of something in order to fully experience its happier side? Why or why not?

_____

_____

_____

_____

Name _____ Date _____

109. Writer and fiction editor for *The New Yorker* Katherine S. White, once wrote that one of the three gardens of winter was "the garden of the mind's eye." What might she mean by that? What are some of the things you might use your imagination for during the winter and why?

_____

_____

_____

_____

110. In Shakespeare's *Love's Labour's Lost,* the character Biron says that there are certain things that make sense in each season. He wouldn't want a rose in winter just like he wouldn't want snow in the spring. Do you ever hope for warm weather in the winter? Why or why not? Do you think having an appropriately snowy winter is important? Why or why not?

_____

_____

_____

_____

Name _____ Date _____

111. In Joni Mitchell's song Urge for Going, she makes it seem like everyone and everything wants to leave when winter closes in. Would you say that's accurate? Why or why not? Have you ever felt like leaving your town for greener pastures during the winter? Why or why not?

_____

_____

_____

_____

_____

112. In the movie *An Affair to Remember*, the character Terry McKay said, "Winter must be cold for those with no warm memories." What does it mean to have a warm memory? Would you agree that people without that kind of memories would act colder? Why or why not?

_____

_____

_____

_____

Name _____ Date _____

113. The narrator in the song California Dreamin' by the Mamas and the
Papas states that he'd be "safe and warm" if he was on the west coast during the coldest months.
Would you rather live in a place that was warm all year round, even if you'd miss out on playing
in the snow? Why or why not?

_____

_____

_____

_____

_____

114. In the famous horror movie *The Shining*, the main character goes crazy when he's cooped up
in a hotel in the middle of nowhere during the winter. Do you ever get restless when you're not
able to go outside in the winter? Why or why not?

_____

_____

_____

_____

Name _____ Date _____

115. The song Early Winter by Gwen Stefani refers to an impending breakup as an "early winter." Do you think of an early winter as an upsetting thing? Why or why not? Why do you think songs and poems often use winter to refer to something negative?

_____

_____

_____

_____

116. The movie *Groundhog Day* shows a grumpy newscaster having to re-live the same winter day over and over again until he gets it right. What would you do if you had to live the same 24 hours over many times in a row during the winter? How would you pass the time and why?

_____

_____

_____

_____

Name _____ Date _____

117. The television show *St. Elsewhere*, a medical drama from the 1980s, ended its series by revealing that the entire universe of the show was the daydream of an autistic child staring into a snow globe. What would you do if you found out that part or all of your life was nothing but a dream? How would you live life differently and why?

_____

_____

_____

_____

118. The movie *The Day After Tomorrow* shows part of the world descending into an ice age with the people having to survive the new landscape. How would your life change if your town became year-long arctic wasteland? Would you consider moving? Why or why not?

_____

_____

_____

_____

Name _____ Date _____

119. In the *Seinfeld* episode The Strike, we are introduced to a winter holiday called Festivus that includes a metal pole and an airing of the grievances. If you could create a winter holiday, what would it be called, what activities would it involve, and would your family enjoy it? Why or why not?

_____

_____

_____

_____

_____

120. In the bleak winter movie *A Simple Plan*, a group of friends and family members find $4 million worth of cash in the middle of nowhere. What would you do if you found that much money that didn't belong to you and why? Would the situation be different if you found the cash with some friends? Why or why not?

_____

_____

_____

_____

_____

Name _____ Date _____

121. One of the most famous American winter events is when George Washington crossed the Delaware River with his troops in 1776. What might it have been like to be under Washington's campaign during such a treacherous journey? Would you have considered deserting the Army like many troops did at that time? Why or why not?

_____

_____

_____

_____

122. In the winter of 1967, the Midwest saw one of the biggest blizzards of all time, which dumped more than two feet of snow with winds exceeding 50 miles per hour just days after tornadoes and temperatures in the 60s. How would you stay safe during such a wintry storm? How would you prepare for it in the first place?

_____

_____

_____

_____

Name _____ Date _____

123. During one of the strangest moments in Winter Olympics history, the ex-husband of figure skater Tonya Harding set up a sneak attack on Harding's rival, Nancy Kerrigan, to try to knock her out of the competition. Imagine that someone tried to sabotage you during a test, game, or sport. How would you respond and why?

_____

_____

_____

_____

_____

124. The winter of 2011-2012 was one of the warmest winters in history. What sorts of things would you do on a warm winter day that would be different from a regular spring or summer day? Would you appreciate the warmer day more in the winter or during another season and why?

_____

_____

_____

_____

Name _____ Date _____

125. When the armies of Napoleon Bonaparte and the French invaded
Russia in 1812, they were unable to handle the Russian winter and eventually had to abandon the
campaign. Imagine that you planned a major event, only to be stopped by tough winter weather.
How would you feel? What might you do instead and why?

_____

_____

_____

_____

126. In an effort to avoid the freezing winter in 1778, British navigator Captain James Cook took
his crew south during an expedition and became the first Brit to find the Hawaiian Islands.
Imagine that you were looking for an object and came upon something much, much better. What
might it be? How would it be better and why?

_____

_____

_____

_____

Name _____ Date _____

127. During the winter of 1873, 15-year-old Chester Greenwood invented the earmuffs to protect his ears. If you could come up with any winter invention, what would it be and why? Do you think it could be as successful as Greenwood's? Why or why not?

_____

_____

_____

_____

128. Norwegians Carl Howelsen and Angell Schmidt introduced ski jumping to the Western United States in 1911 in Hot Sulphur Springs, Colorado, spurring an extremely popular ski industry in the mountainous state. What would it be like if you could introduce something in a foreign land? How would people treat you? How would you feel and why?

_____

_____

_____

_____

Name _____ Date _____

129. In the 1988 Olympics, the Caribbean island of Jamaica sent its first representatives to the Winter Olympics as part of the bobsled team event. What do you think winter would be like for you if you'd only previously experienced a tropical beach environment? What challenges might you face and why?

_____

_____

_____

_____

130. *Snow White and the Seven Dwarfs* was released into theaters in December 1937, and it was the first full-length animated movie. Imagine that you were the first person to do or create something. What might that thing be and why? How would you feel after doing it?

_____

_____

_____

_____

Name _____ Date _____

131. In China, the Dongzhi Festival is a Winter Solstice festival in which people eat brightly colored rice balls and worship their ancestors. Which of your ancestors might you want to honor during such a holiday and why? Do you think it's important to remember your family's past? Why or why not?

_____

_____

_____

_____

132. Sadeh, a Persian festival, celebrates fire and its ability to keep away frost, cold, and dark. How important might fire have been in your life if you lived over 100 years ago and why? Does fire still play a role in your life today? Why or why not?

_____

_____

_____

_____

Name _____ Date _____

133. On January 13, some Ukrainian, Belarusian, and Russian cultures celebrate Malanka, a night of playing pranks, acting out plays, and dressing men in women's clothing. What would such a festival be like in your neighborhood? Would you enjoy it? Why or why not?

_____

_____

_____

_____

134. Canada's Quebec City holds a Winter Carnival every February that is filled with music, art, parades and dogsled races. What would your life be like if you needed a dogsled to get to school every day? How would you take care of the dogs? What would your sled look like?

_____

_____

_____

_____

Name _____ Date _____

135. One of the largest international snow sculpture contests can be found on Japan's Hokkaido island in the city of Sapporo every February. If you wanted to win the Yuki Matsuri contest, what would you build and why? Who would you recruit to help you?

_____

_____

_____

_____

136. Up Helly Aa is a winter festival held in the Shetland Islands, United Kingdom, in which residents dress up like Vikings and burn down a replica ancient ship. Imagine you could bring a real Viking from the past to see this festival. What might he think about it and why?

_____

_____

_____

_____

Name _____ Date _____

137. During the winter, Siberia's 400-mile Lake Baikal completely freezes over, giving way to major festivals taking part on top of the ice. If all of the water in the world froze over for a week and you could travel anywhere by car or bus, where would you go and why? What would it be like traveling on the slick, icy, former lakes, rivers, and oceans?

_____

_____

_____

_____

138. In France, the story of Santa Claus is slightly different: children put out their shoes to collect presents and add beet greens to feed the donkey that Santa rides. Would you want to try out how different cultures celebrate Christmas and other holidays? Why or why not?

_____

_____

_____

_____

Name _____ Date _____

139. The winter holiday Bodhi Day, a part of Buddhist cultures, is less about food and celebrations and more about sitting and thinking. What kind of ideas could you come up with if you sat and thought more often? Do you think it's important to have some quiet time to yourself? Why or why not?

_____

_____

_____

_____

140. Diwali is a major holiday in India that includes a festival of lights, food, and other celebrations. The winter holiday is celebrated in different ways depending on what region of India you live in. What tweaks would you add to American winter holidays if you had a choice? Would these changes catch on? Why or why not?

_____

_____

_____

_____

Name _____ Date _____

141. If you could create a piece of artwork to represent winter, what would it look like and why? What kind of materials would you use? What would people think if it got put into a museum and why?

_____

_____

_____

_____

_____

142. You've discovered a time capsule full of old pictures and newspaper clippings of the people who lived in your house during the winter of 50 years ago. Describe all of the contents of the time capsule. What might you learn about winter in your town from this discovery and why?

_____

_____

_____

_____

Name _____ Date _____

143. You've been entered into a winter obstacle race with an exciting first place prize. What are some of the winter-themed obstacles? Which might you have the most trouble with and why? What's the prize and do you win it?

_____

_____

_____

_____

_____

144. Which of the following competitions would your family be most likely to win and why: winter holiday house decorating, skiing relay race, ice hockey match, or partner figure skating contest?

_____

_____

_____

_____

_____

Name _____ Date _____

145. Create a made-up story using the following words: icicles, snow
blower, frostbitten, and triumph.

_____

_____

_____

_____

146. What are some ways in which your winter diet is different from your summer diet? In which
season do you eat more healthfully and why?

_____

_____

_____

_____

Name _____ Date _____

147. How would your winter change if you had a heated hot tub in your backyard? How would you use this toasty device to melt away your winter blues? Which of your friends might come over to use it and why?

_____

_____

_____

_____

_____

148. Imagine that you and a friend or family member have started a business shoveling neighbors' driveways for a fee. How much money would you charge, how long would each driveway take, and how difficult would it be? How would you feel to be working in the freezing cold and why?

_____

_____

_____

_____

_____

Name _____ Date _____

149. While digging up snow in your backyard, you find a cave person completely frozen in ice! What happens next? Are you happy about the end result of your find? Why or why not?

_____

_____

_____

_____

150. Describe your ideal snow day. Where would you be, what would you be doing and who would you be with? How would such a day make you feel and why?

_____

_____

_____

_____

Name _____ Date _____

151. The poet E.E. Cummings once wrote that "the earth laughs in flowers." Would you agree with Cummings? What are some other ways that the earth might laugh and why? How does the earth laughing differ from the way humans laugh and why?

_____

_____

_____

_____

152. "No spring skips its turn," according to author and journalist Hal Borland. How would the world be different if spring did skip its turn? What would be the parts of spring you'd miss the most and why?

_____

_____

_____

_____

Name _____ Date _____

153. Author Geoffrey B. Charlesworth spoke of spring as if it were an orchestra. If spring was an orchestra, what instruments do you think each different type of animal and plant would play and why? What would such spring music sound like and why?

_____

_____

_____

_____

154. April is like a green traffic light that makes the world think "Go" according to poet and essayist Christopher Morley. What are some ways that people "go" during the spring? What are some ways the other seasons make people stop and why?

_____

_____

_____

_____

Name _____ Date _____

155. Mark Twain and many other writers have discussed the concept of
spring fever as a feeling that makes you want to go out, have fun, and fall in love. What do you
think spring fever would feel like and why? In what ways would someone with spring fever act
differently and why?

_____

_____

_____

_____

_____

156. Margaret Atwood, an author and environmental activist, once said that at the end of a spring
day "you should smell like dirt." Imagine that you have planted a beautiful spring garden with
your family and you need to tend to it every day. How would you make time for the garden?
Would you have to remove any technological things from your schedule? Why or why not?

_____

_____

_____

_____

Name _____ Date _____

157. According to a Chinese proverb, plants recognize spring sooner than humans do. What do you think the first sign of spring is for a plant and why? Aside from the calendar, what is a sign that spring has come for you and why? How do you feel when you realize it's finally spring?

_____

_____

_____

_____

_____

158. Chilean poet and diplomat Pablo Neruda said that "you can cut all the flowers but you cannot keep spring from coming." Why do you think some people remain grumpy even when it's beautiful outside during the spring? If you were feeling unhappy during the spring, what would you do to snap out of it and why?

_____

_____

_____

_____

Name _____ Date _____

159. It's important to enjoy how the seasons change from one to another as opposed to simply being in love with spring, according to writer George Santayana. What are some ways you can love the other three seasons as much as you enjoy spring? Would your life be different if you enjoyed the weather and the transitions throughout all the seasons? Why or why not?

_____

_____

_____

_____

160. Wallace Stevens, an American poet, said that spring prepares everyone an annual surprise. Imagine that you did in fact receive a major surprise every spring. What would this year's surprise be and why? What would be some of the surprises the season could hold for you in the future and why?

_____

_____

_____

_____

Name _____ Date _____

161. Actor Robin Williams once said that "spring is nature's way of saying, 'Let's party!'" Would you agree with him? Why or why not? What are some ways that nature parties during the spring? Does nature enjoy itself? Why or why not?

_____

_____

_____

_____

162. In the song Suddenly It's Spring, which was famously sung by Frank Sinatra, the narrator feels young and free and starts dancing because it's spring. Has spring ever made you feel the same way? Why or why not? What about spring might cause someone to be that happy and why?

_____

_____

_____

_____

Name _____ Date _____

163. *The Secret Garden*, a children's novel that has been made into multiple movie adaptations, shows that having a garden and growing things can be very healing. Who in your life might be happier and healthier if they had a garden to grow and why? What are some aspects of having a garden that you might enjoy and why?

_____

_____

_____

_____

164. The classic 1960 spring break movie *Where the Boys Are* is set in Ft. Lauderdale, Florida. The movie inspired thousands to visit the city the following years, which is an example of life imitating art. What are some ways that movies and television shows have inspired people in real life to do things? Have you ever been motivated to do something because of a movie? Why or why not?

_____

_____

_____

_____

Name _____ Date _____

165. The movie *Bambi* shows a springtime in which all the animals fall in
love, or as they call it, become twitter-pated. What do you think it means to become twitter-pated?
Have you ever been twitter-pated? If so, what did it feel like, and if not, how do you think you
would react and why?

_____

_____

_____

_____

166. *Spring, Summer, Fall, Winter...and Spring* is a movie about a young Buddhist apprentice and
how he learns about life cycles from his master. Do you think it's important to be kind to plants
and animals? Why or why not?

_____

_____

_____

_____

Name _____ Date _____

167. In the movie *It Happens Every Spring*, a scientist accidentally comes up with a chemical that makes baseballs unhittable. He uses the chemical to become a successful pitcher until he runs out. Do you think it would be fair to use a substance to get an advantage in a sport? Why or why not? Would it be considered cheating? Why or why not?

_____

_____

_____

_____

_____

168. In the movie *The Lorax*, based on the Dr. Seuss classic, the spring is completely treeless because the trees were all chopped down to make the Once-ler a fortune. What would you do if a greedy company began cutting down all the trees? How would you try to convince the company's president that trees are important? Would you succeed? Why or why not?

_____

_____

_____

_____

Name _____ Date _____

169. A colony of ants is oppressed by some evil grasshoppers in the classic Pixar film, *A Bug's Life*. Why is it important to stand up for yourself and what you believe in? Do you think there are places in the world where people are oppressed by the powerful and ruthless? Why or why not?

_____

_____

_____

_____

170. Set in the beautiful, green countryside, the movie *Pollyanna* follows the life of a girl who learns to be perpetually optimistic despite a difficult life and a crippling injury. Do you think optimism is important? Why or why not? What benefits might an optimist have that a pessimist wouldn't have and why?

_____

_____

_____

_____

Name _____ Date _____

171. Geoffrey Chaucer's *The Canterbury Tales*, which was set during a spring pilgrimage, was one of the great early contributions to English literature, written in the late 1300s. What are some words you use today that would not have been around over 700 years ago? Do you think you'd have a tough time talking to people who lived back then? Why or why not?

_____

_____

_____

_____

172. The first spring training, a two-month out-of-town training period in which players try out for Major League Baseball teams, started in the spring of 1870 in New Orleans. Imagine that you started the first two months of school touring around the country. Where would you want to go and why? What might you learn during your city-by-city tour?

_____

_____

_____

_____

Name _____ Date _____

173. The tradition of spring cleaning may have started with ancient Jewish, Chinese, and Iranian cultures cleaning for various holidays and traditions. What are some other traditions in your household that might have started hundreds or thousands of years ago? How would it be different to do those chores before electricity and why?

_____

_____

_____

_____

174. Spring break is a wild and crazy time for people in high school and college, and the most recent tradition may have stemmed from the city of Fort Lauderdale starting a College Coaches' Swim Forum in 1938. What is the largest party you've ever been to? Did you enjoy it? Why or why not?

_____

_____

_____

_____

Name _____ Date _____

175. In the spring of 1912, the RMS Titanic, a ship carrying thousands of people, ran into an iceberg at full speed and sank. The crew had received warnings of the icy waters but failed to listen. Why do you think it's important to listen when someone gives you advice? Have you ever failed to listen to important advice? What happened and why?

_____

_____

_____

_____

_____

176. The word April means "to open." What are some of the things that open during April? If you could open a new shop or business during the spring, what would it be and why?

_____

_____

_____

_____

_____

Name _____ Date _____

177. The first Kentucky Derby was run in the spring of 1875. Create a conversation between two thoroughbred horses getting ready to compete in the biggest event in their lives. Would they be scared? Why or why not?

_____

_____

_____

_____

_____

178. March Madness, a spring college basketball tournament with 68 teams competing for first place, expanded from eight teams in 1939, to 64 in 1985, to 68 in 2011. Imagine that you played for the last place in the tournament. What would you feel like going against the toughest team in the nation? Would you have a chance of winning? Why or why not?

_____

_____

_____

_____

Name _____ Date _____

179. Before the Gregorian Calendar was introduced, April 1 used to be part of the new year celebration. When it changed to January 1 in France in the 1580s, some people didn't believe it and were labeled "April fools." Imagine that someone told you something you couldn't believe. What would it be? Why wouldn't you believe it?

_____

_____

_____

_____

180. The first Mother's Day was celebrated in 1914 and quickly became about cards, gifts and other commercial practices. Do you think gifts and other tangible items are necessary on Mother's Day? Why or why not?

_____

_____

_____

_____

Name _____ Date _____

181. The Cherry Blossom Festival in Japan runs all spring long, depending on when the beautiful flowers blossom throughout the country. Imagine what it would be like to travel through Japan to experience every town's individual festival. How do you think the towns would differ from each other and why? How would seeing the flowers blossom make you feel and why?

_____

_____

_____

_____

_____

182. Thailand is the site of the Songkran Water Festival in which people, statues, and even elephants are enlisted in a three-day-long water fight. If you had a giant water fight in your town, who would you want on your team and why? Would your team be successful? Why or why not?

_____

_____

_____

_____

_____

Name _____ Date _____

183. In April in cities around the world, the celebration of Critical Mass is
a disruptive occasion in which hundreds of bicyclists ride down the streets of major cities in packs
to disrupt traffic. What would it be like to bike in this mass of people? What do you think is the
purpose of this celebration and why?

_____

_____

_____

_____

_____

184. The spring is the season for cheese-rolling in Gloucester, United Kingdom as individuals and
teams compete in races to roll wheels of cheese down a hill the fastest. What would you enjoy the
most about watching silly people roll cheese down a hill while tumbling themselves? Would you
more enjoy watching the people or eating the cheese afterward? Why?

_____

_____

_____

_____

Name _____ Date _____

185. Some of the most famous film celebrities will be on hand at the Cannes Film Festival in Cannes, France, during the spring. What would it be like to be an acclaimed and beloved film director? Which movie star would you enjoy working with the most and why?

_____

_____

_____

_____

186. The Feria Del Caballo in Seville, Spain celebrates horses, bullfights and traditional Spanish traditions for two weeks in April and May. If you were in Spain for the festival, would you watch the bullfights? Why or why not? Would you enjoy life as a bullfighter? Why or why not?

_____

_____

_____

_____

Name _____ Date _____

187. In the Philippines, the residents love their buffaloes so much that they hold the Pulilan Carabao festival in which they give the mammals a shower, a shave, and a parade. What would your family life be like if you owned and took care of a buffalo? What chores would you have to add to your list?

_____

_____

_____

_____

_____

188. A wild carnival in Copenhagen, Denmark pulls in approximately 200,000 people each spring to show off different kinds of dancing and music from around the world. Imagine that you were an amazing dancer, the best in your town or school. How would you use these dancing abilities and why? What would people think of your skills and why?

_____

_____

_____

_____

_____

Name _____ Date _____

189. In Krakow, Poland, the Lajkonik Festival celebrates a major military victory with a re-enactment and an all-night party. What are some of the military victories we celebrate in the United States? Do you think it's important to remember our successes? Why or why not?

_____

_____

_____

_____

190. There are multiple comedy festivals throughout the spring around the world including the Cat Laughs Kilkenny in Ireland and the Melbourne International Comedy Festival in Australia. What do you think it takes to be a funny comedian? Who is the funniest person you know personally? Do you think that person could ever be a professional comedian? Why or why not?

_____

_____

_____

_____

Name _____ Date _____

191. Create a made-up story using the following words: garden, rabbit, aroma, and picnic.

_____

_____

_____

_____

_____

192. What is the most important aspect of spring to you and why? What is the most important part of spring to your parents and why? Do you think the things you like about spring will change as you get older? Why or why not?

_____

_____

_____

_____

Name _____ Date _____

193. Some schools have a Spring Fling dance in which everyone is invited. Would you want to attend? Why or why not? What would you enjoy the most about the dance and what would you enjoy the least? Why?

_____

_____

_____

_____

194. After some hemming and hawing, you decide to attend the Spring Fling. What will you wear to the dance, what types of dances will you do, and whom will you dance with? Which of your friends would have the best dance moves and why?

_____

_____

_____

_____

Name _____ Date _____

195. As part of a challenge, you will participate in 24 outdoor activities in 24 hours (1 hour for each). What are some of the sports you would play? What would be the toughest aspects of the challenge and why?

_____

_____

_____

_____

_____

196. If you couldn't go outside for an entire week during the heart of the spring, what would you miss the most about the outdoors and why? What would you do inside to pass the time and why?

_____

_____

_____

_____

Name _____ Date _____

197. Trees can live for a particularly long time, even longer than humans.
Describe what a tree might think upon watching a human grow up all the way from infancy to old age.

_____

_____

_____

_____

_____

198. Spring is often referred to as a key part of the life cycle. Do you think it's important that the lives of organisms are cyclical? Why or why not? How do you think it would feel to be an animal or insect with a very short life cycle and why?

_____

_____

_____

_____

Name _____ Date _____

199. What are some things that you think about during the spring that you might not think about during other seasons and why? When do you do your most thinking during the day and why is that your best thinking time?

_____

_____

_____

_____

_____

200. Many creatures we talk about during the spring, like birds, bees, and squirrels, base most of their actions in instinct. Do you think it's important that humans have the ability to go beyond instinct? Why or why not? What are some ways you use reason in your daily life?

_____

_____

_____

_____

Extra Page

Name _____ Date _____

_____

_____

_____

_____

_____

_____

_____

_____

_____

_____

_____

ABOUT THE AUTHOR

Bryan Cohen is a writer, actor and director who grew up in Dresher, Pennsylvania just outside of Philadelphia. He graduated from the University of North Carolina at Chapel Hill with degrees in English and Dramatic Art along with a minor in Creative Writing. His books on writing prompts and writing motivation have sold over 15,000 copies and they include *1,000 Creative Writing Prompts: Ideas for Blogs, Scripts, Stories and More, 1,000 Character Writing Prompts: Villains, Heroes and Hams for Scripts, Stories and More, 500 Writing Prompts for Kids: First Grade through Fifth Grade, 1,000 Character Writing Prompts: Villains, Heroes and Hams for Scripts, Stories and More* and *The Post-College Guide to Happiness*. Cohen continues to produce and perform plays and films in between his books and freelance writing work. He lives in Chicago.

Made in the USA
San Bernardino, CA
01 September 2015